# CHRISTMAS PROGRAMS for Children

Compiled by
**Brynn Robertson**

**Standard**
PUBLISHING
*Bringing The Word to Life*

Cincinnati, Ohio

Permission is granted to reproduce these programs
for ministry purposes only—not for resale.

Scripture taken from the HOLY BIBLE,
NEW INTERNATIONAL VERSION®. NIV®.
Copyright © 1973, 1978, 1984 by International Bible Society.
Used by permission of Zondervan. All rights reserved.

Standard Publishing
Cincinnati, Ohio.
A division of Standex International Corporation
© 2006 by Standard Publishing

All rights reserved.
Printed in the United States of America

ISBN 0-7847-1646-3

# Contents

## Christmas

Wish List .................................................................................. 4
    John Cosper
No Jesus, No Christmas ........................................................ 5
    Brett Parker
The Ad Campaign ................................................................ 10
    John Cosper
C-H-R-I-S-T-M-A-S .............................................................. 12
    Alyce Pickett
Christmas Dress Rehearsal ................................................. 13
    John Cosper
Christmas While You Wait ................................................... 17
    Susan Sundwall
From the Manger ................................................................. 20
    Dixie Phillips
Santa's Christmas Tree ....................................................... 23
    John Cosper
Silent Night Surprise ........................................................... 28
    Brett Parker
A Donkey's Story ................................................................. 31
    Alyce Pickett
Prayer Mail .......................................................................... 32
    Paula Reed
The Christmas Toys ............................................................. 36
    John Cosper

## Thanksgiving

Turkey Trouble .................................................................... 40
    Brett Parker
The Turkey Thanksgiving .................................................... 43
    John Cosper
Thankful for Pie ................................................................... 46
    Susan Sundwall

# Wish List
by John Cosper

**Summary:** A little girl remembers how Christmas used to be all about getting gifts, until she learned the true spirit is giving.
**Character:**
GIRL—young girl appearing to look about 4 or 5
**Setting:** bare stage
**Costume:** modern-day little girl's clothing

GIRL: When I was a really littler kid, there was only one thing I wanted for Christmas: a dollie! I begged my mommy and daddy until I got her.

But then you know what happened? I grew up. Yup, and when I was about, mmmmm, 4, I wanted a grown-up present. I wanted a Pink Pretty Princess Super Bike 2000. All year long, I begged my mommy and daddy for the bike, and guess what? I got it! And I got out and saw the world.

But then, a long time later, when I was about, oh, 6, I learned about a present even better than a bike, or a dollie. I heard about it in church. I also learned it was the very first and bestest Christmas present ever. Know what it was? It was a baby, but not like my dollie. It was a real one, and His name was Jesus. He was God's only Son. I asked my mommy and daddy for Jesus, but this time, they told me I had to ask Jesus himself to come into my heart. And you know what? He did! Yup! *[knocks on chest]* He's right in there. He keeps me company all day.

But you know what? It's been a year since I got Jesus, and there's still one more thing I want for Christmas. See, I've been hearing that there are kids in the world that don't know about Jesus. Matter of fact, there are some kids in the world that have never heard about Christmas.
So I asked my mommy and my daddy, and you know what they said? They said Jesus was a gift that only I could give. Jesus wants me to tell everyone I know about Him. Can you believe that? I told them they were crazy, but then I got to thinking. Now I have Jesus, and now, I can go and tell everyone that Jesus loves them.

*[Blackout.]*

# No Jesus, No Christmas
by Brett Parker

**Summary:** Everyone in the Taylor family is getting ready to go see Santa at the mall! The only problem is that the family is taking a little bit longer to get ready than Mr. Taylor expected.

**Characters:**
Mr. Taylor—middle-aged man, a little high-strung, best if played by a teen or adult
Mrs. Taylor—middle-aged woman, calm and cheerful, best if played by a teen or adult
Jason—boy about 8 years old, brother of Ashley
Ashley—girl about 6 years old, sister of Jason
**Setting:** living room of the Taylor family home
**Props:** a plate or tray for Christmas cookies, newspaper, coffee mug, a watch, small living room table and seats for 4, a roll of paper or a long piece of paper for a Christmas list, a coat
**Costumes:** modern-day clothing

*The skit opens with Mr. Taylor waltzing into the living room, coffee mug in hand, cheerfully whistling to the tune of "Jingle Bells." He sits down in his chair, picks up the newspaper and begins to read it. After a moment he glances at his watch. He is shocked to realize what time it is. He runs over to the side and appears to be looking out a window.*

Mr. Taylor: Oh no! That snow is really coming down! We've got to get going! *[He looks around and notices that no one else is in the room with him. He walks to back of the room and looks up the staircase.]* Honey? Kids? Hurry up! If we don't leave soon we're going to miss Santa!

*[Mrs. Taylor enters living room carrying a plate of Christmas cookies and sets them down on a small table in the middle of the room.]*

Mrs. Taylor: Oh relax, dear. Santa will be at the mall all day long. I'm sure everyone will get a chance to see him.
Mr. Taylor: Not at this pace. *[He glances at his watch again.]* By the time we fight through traffic in the snow to get to the mall, Santa will probably be on his lunch break. And you know it's only a few days before Christmas. Who knows how long the line to see him will be after that?!

Mrs. Taylor: Now, dear. Please just be calm. You know how excited the kids are to see Santa. I'm sure they don't mind the traffic or waiting in the lines.

Mr. Taylor: Yes, but I do. *[pauses for a moment, and then notices that the kids are still not anywhere to be seen]* Jason! Ashley! Let's go!

*[Jason enters the room running, jumping and acting completely wild.]*

Jason: Yippee! Santa, here I come! This is going to be great! I've been looking forward to this for a whole year!

Mrs. Taylor: *[laughing at Jason's enthusiasm]* Well, I'm glad you're excited! Do you know what you're going to ask Santa for Christmas?

Jason: *[his eyes get wide and a huge smile comes across his face]* Do I? You better believe I do! I've got it all figured out, Mom. I'm asking Santa for the new, the awesome, Super Power Space Soldier action figure, complete with a laser gun, turbo charged utility belt, and his own personal spaceship! Not only that, but he is able to leap, run, crawl, jump, fly and perform Ninja moves! *[He lets out a loud Ninja scream and starts karate chopping Mr. Taylor.]*

Mr. Taylor: Yeah, yeah. Well, Sport, if we don't hurry you won't get a chance to tell Santa anything. Where's your sister? *[loudly]* Ashley?!

Ashley: *[She happily skips into room, singing "Santa Claus Is Coming to Town." She has with her a large roll of paper; singing with different lyrics]* He sees me when I'm sleeping, he knows when I'm awake! He knows if *I've* been bad or good, and *I have* been good for goodness sake!

Mr. Taylor: There you are, Ashley. Are you ready? What took you so long?

Ashley: Well, of course I'm ready *now*, Daddy. I couldn't leave before I finished writing my Christmas list to Santa.

Mrs. Taylor: *[smiling]* And what are *you* asking from Santa this year?

Ashley: *[clears her throat]* Well, as you all know, I have been on my best behavior for the last three weeks. I have cleaned my room *everyday*, eaten *all* the food on my dinner plate each night—even the broccoli—and I even helped my teacher erase the board last week. So, because I have been *really* good, I made my list extra long this year. *[She drops one end of the roll of paper, her list, and lets it roll across the room. Everyone is astonished to see how long her list is.]*

Mrs. Taylor: My, that certainly looks like a long list, Ashley.

Mr. Taylor: Come on, Ashley. You can read it to us in the car. The snow is coming down really hard now.

JASON: Yeah! We don't have time, now! We're going to miss . . .
ASHLEY: *[interrupts JASON]* First, I am asking for the new Jet Ski Barbie. Next, I would like a new pink lunch box, complete with thermos, handle, and cup holder. I also want a make-up kit, and nurse's kit, a sled, a new hairbrush, an easy-bake oven, a cotton candy machine, a bubblegum machine, a doll house, a pony, a puppy, a kitten, *two* bunny rabbits, a gold-fish and a turtle.
MRS. TAYLOR: *[somewhat disappointed]* Goodness, that IS quite a long list, sweetie. Are you sure you need all of those things?
JASON: Honestly Ashley, what are you trying to do? Turn our house into a zoo?
ASHLEY: We might as well. Your room is already a pig sty! *[She rubs her knuckles on his head and begins to run away, laughing]*
JASON: *[chases after ASHLEY]* Is not!
ASHLEY: Is too! *[makes pig sounds]*
MR. TAYLOR: *[becoming upset]* Hey! We DO NOT have time for this! Now I'm going to go start the car, and when I get back everyone had better be friendly and ready to go! *[puts on his coat and then exits]*
JASON: *[chases ASHLEY again]* Is not times one hundred!
ASHLEY: Is too times one million!
JASON: Is not times a gazillion!
ASHLEY: That's not even a real number!
JASON: Is too!
ASHLEY: Is not!
MRS. TAYLOR: Please, kids. Try to be nice to each other. It's Christmastime. *[walking over to look outside]* Wow. It really is snowing hard! *[sees MR. TAYLOR coming back]* Here comes your dad.

*[JASON and ASHLEY quit chasing each other and try to look like they are getting ready. MR. TAYLOR quickly enters. He shivers and takes off his coat. He has a look of disappointment on his face]*

MR. TAYLOR: Well, everyone, I am afraid I have some bad news. It looks like we are snowed in.
JASON: What?!
ASHLEY: Isn't there anything we can do?
MR. TAYLOR: I'm sorry, kids. There's just too much snow. I can't even get the car out of the driveway. It looks like we're stuck here for a while. At least until the roads clear up.
MRS. TAYLOR: Oh, dear. I'm so sorry everyone.

**JASON:** No Santa?

**MR. TAYLOR:** I'm afraid not, Jason.

**JASON:** Without telling Santa what I want, he'll never know what to bring me! That means no Santa, no Christmas. *[turns to ASHLEY]* This is all your fault! If you wouldn't have taken so long with your Christmas list, we could have gotten to see Santa!

**ASHLEY:** My fault?! *[stuttering]* Why . . . I have never in all my life . . . How rude!

**MR. TAYLOR:** Hey! *[becoming angry again]* What did I say about arguing?! There will be no arguing! This is becoming a very stressful day!

**MRS. TAYLOR:** Dear, please, calm down. Have a seat. *[motions for MR. TAYLOR to sit in his chair]* Jason, Ashley. You too. Sit, sit. *[waits for everyone to have a seat and puts her hands on her hips]* Does anyone here know the real meaning of Christmas? Have you forgotten what Christmas is really all about?

**JASON:** Santa?

**ASHLEY:** Presents?

**MRS. TAYLOR:** No, it's not about Christmas trees, or going to the mall, Santa, or even presents. *[smiling bright]* It's about Jesus! On Christmas, we celebrate the birth of Jesus. Without him, there wouldn't be a Christmas. It's not "No Santa, no Christmas," Jason. It's "No Jesus, no Christmas." We don't need Christmas gifts or toys to have Christmas. All we need is Jesus.

**MR. TAYLOR:** *[realizing that he shouldn't be so angry]* Your mom is right, kids. I think I missed the meaning of Christmas too. I got so wrapped up in getting you guys to the mall to see Santa that I forgot the whole point of Christmas, to celebrate Jesus' birthday. And I am so lucky that I get to celebrate with all of you! I'm sorry that I got so mad and yelled.

**ASHLEY:** I'm sorry too. I guess my list is a little too long, huh? I don't really need *all* of those things on my list. Christmas shouldn't be about getting a lot of presents.

**JASON:** Yeah, I forgot what Christmas was about too. I was so set on seeing Santa that I wouldn't let anything get in the way. I'm sorry I was so mean to you, Ashley.

**ASHLEY:** It's all right, Jason. From now on we should try to be nice to each other. And not just because Santa Claus is watching, but because Jesus wants us to.

**MRS. TAYLOR:** Now that's the Christmas spirit!

**MR. TAYLOR:** It certainly is! I'm so proud of you two! *[looks at MRS.*

TAYLOR] And you too, Mom. Thanks for reminding us what Christmas should really be about. Group hug! *[they all run over to MRS. TAYLOR and engage in a group hug]*
**MRS. TAYLOR:** Thank you, everyone!
**MR. TAYLOR:** *[glances outside]* Aw. I still feel bad about the snow, though. How are we going to get these lists to Santa?
**MRS. TAYLOR:** Why don't we e-mail them to Santa?
**JASON:** We can do that?
**MRS. TAYLOR:** Of course we can!
**ASHLEY:** All right!
**JASON:** Awesome! *[gives ASHLEY a high five]*
**MR. TAYLOR:** Come on, kids! I'll help you write them! *[exits, followed by JASON and ASHLEY]*
**MRS. TAYLOR:** *[looks up]* Happy Birthday, Jesus! *[Exits. Blackout.]*

# The Ad Campaign
by John Cosper

**Summary:** A zealous angel wants to arrange a mass media campaign to announce the birth of Jesus but another explains God's simple plan for revealing Christ to the world.

**Characters:**
MICHAEL—angel
DARRELL—angel
**Setting:** Heaven
**Costumes:** angel robes

*MICHAEL and DARRELL enter.*

**MICHAEL:** Well, Darrell, we're at T-minus 20 hours to the big event. Are you ready?
**DARRELL:** Ready? I was made for this, pal!
**MICHAEL:** Weren't we all?
**DARRELL:** I can't believe the day is here.
**MICHAEL:** I know. The Son of God is about to enter creation and bridge the gap between God and man!!
**DARRELL:** And we're just the guys to tell the whole world about it!
**MICHAEL:** You bet we—Wait, what are we gonna do?
**DARRELL:** Why, kick off the marketing campaign for Jesus, of course!
**MICHAEL:** What marketing campaign? I never heard anything about this.
**DARRELL:** Not to worry. I've already mapped the whole thing out. First, we start with the teaser.
**MICHAEL:** Teaser?
**DARRELL:** The star, of course. It's just a sample, a taste, a small sign of things to come—something that'll get people talking. Then, after a month or so, we start with the billboards.
**MICHAEL:** Billboards?
**DARRELL:** That's right. I'm thinking one or two on every major route in Israel, plus a few extras inside the big cities like Jerusalem. At first, they'll have simple quotes from the prophets. Something like, "To us a child is born!" Maybe with a picture of the star.
**MICHAEL:** I don't know . . .
**DARRELL:** You're right. We'll put the kid's picture on the billboards. And once those signs are up, we start with the radio spots.
**MICHAEL:** Radio spots? What are you talking about?

**DARRELL:** You're right. No one listens to the radio any more. We'll advertise on television—a 30-second spot in prime time, featuring the angelic host singing of His birth! Of course, once He's old enough to talk, we'll send Him on the chat shows.

**MICHAEL:** Darrell . . .

**DARRELL:** Not the smutty shows, though. I'm thinking the legit morning news programs, and maybe one of the prime time shows. Like *60 Minutes*.

**MICHAEL:** Darrell! Television won't be invented for another two millennia!

**DARRELL:** So?

**MICHAEL:** That's gonna be a little late for your little advertising campaign.

**DARRELL:** Little? Michael, this is no little ad campaign! This is the biggest moment in history since . . . well, since EVER!

**MICHAEL:** And God's got it all planned out already.

**DARRELL:** He has?

**MICHAEL:** Yes.

**DARRELL:** Well, don't leave me in suspense!! What's He got planned? Billboards? Fliers? Or simply a blimp to fly over the colisseum?

**MICHAEL:** One star and one sign.

**DARRELL:** And?

**MICHAEL:** And that's it. One star and one sign.

**DARRELL:** That's it?

**MICHAEL:** That's all He needs.

**DARRELL:** That can't be!! What if people aren't around to see the star? What if it's cloudy? And how is everyone going to see one sign?

**MICHAEL:** Darrell, this is God's Son. He's had a long time to prepare for it. And if the hand that made all creation only needs a star and a sign . . . I'd say he's got everything He needs.

*[Blackout.]*

# C-H-R-I-S-T-M-A-S
by Alyce Pickett

**Summary:** A poetic reading about the reason we celebrate the holiday season.
**Characters:**
    9 children for speaking parts
**Props:** 9 pieces of poster board, each with a letter of the word *Christmas*

*Children walk on stage, each holding a letter. When in place, children hold the letters in front of them to spell CHRISTMAS.*

**C:** is for Christ child . . . Jesus was His name.
**H:** is for Heaven, His home before He came.
**R:** our Redeemer, born in a stable dim,
**I:** is the inn that had no room for Him.
**S:** is the star showing men the way.
**T:** is tidings shepherds heard that day.
**M:** is mother, of the child with halo bright,
**A:** is angels who came in shining light,
**S:** is for Savior . . . the one God sent that night.

*[Blackout.]*

# Christmas Dress Rehearsal
by John Cosper

**Summary:** QUENTIN is a hand puppet who is directing GABRIEL in his part in the upcoming announcement of Jesus' birth.
**Characters:**
GABRIEL—angel, confused about his part in the Christmas story
QUENTIN—angel, directs GABRIEL (actually a hand puppet)
VANESSA—angel who helps GABRIEL (actually a hand puppet)
**Setting:** Heaven, needs to have a table with a white sheet covering it so the puppets can come in and out of the scene
**Props:** 2 hand puppets that look like angels, bandage for puppeteer's hand, tiny coffee mug for QUENTIN to drink, script for GABRIEL and small-sized script for QUENTIN (puppet), sound of trumpets
**Costumes:** white robes for angel and puppets

*GABRIEL enters.*

**GABRIEL:** *[hesitant, nervous, raises hand as if to block a spotlight from his face]* Uhhh, hey. Do not be afraid. I bring you good . . . I bring you good . . . Line.

*[VANESSA pops up.]*

**VANESSA:** Good tidings!
**GABRIEL:** Oh! Good tidings of great joy that will be for . . . for . . . Line.
**VANESSA:** All people! *[pops down]*
**GABRIEL:** Right! All people. For unto you this day, in the city of David . . . Line.

*[QUENTIN and VANESSA pop up.]*

**QUENTIN:** Cut, cut, cut. Gabriel, are you feeling OK?
**GABRIEL:** Me? Yeah, I'm fine.
**QUENTIN:** Is that so. Well let me ask you something. *[holds up script]* You see this script?
**GABRIEL:** Yes.
**QUENTIN:** Does this look like a chicken to you?
**GABRIEL:** No.
**QUENTIN:** Then how come you keep fowling it up?

GABRIEL: *[laughs]* Ha, ha, that was good.
QUENTIN: Wish I could say the same for you. Now, Gabe, baby, this is a very important announcement. You can't just go out there and stumble over it.
GABRIEL: I know, Quentin. I'm sorry. I'll keep working on this.
QUENTIN: See that you do. Keep running lines with him. I'm going to drink some coffee.

*[QUENTIN steps over to the side. He picks up an empty coffee cup from out of view and lifts it to drink.]*

GABRIEL: Coffee? Can a puppet drink coffee?
VANESSA: Wouldn't that burn the puppeteer's arm?

*[A scream is heard offstage. GABRIEL and VANESSA look around. QUENTIN looks down.]*

QUENTIN: Sorry!!!

*[The puppeteer lifts an empty fist into view and shakes it.]*

QUENTIN: I'll be back. *[to his puppeteer]* You big baby!
GABRIEL: Vanessa, what am I going to do? I want to do a good job.
VANESSA: What seems to be the problem.
GABRIEL: I don't know. I guess I just can't get the motivation.
VANESSA: Ohhhh, I see. Maybe I can help out. Let's take a look at the speech.
GABRIEL: Sure. OK. First, "Do not be afraid."
VANESSA: Right, that's standard opening for an angel's speech.
GABRIEL: Oh? Why is that?
VANESSA: Yeah. Imagine you're a human, minding your own business, and suddenly a figure in white appears, floating in midair. Wouldn't that scare you?
GABRIEL: Ah, good thinking. Next. "I bring you good tidings of great joy that will be for all people." What's that mean?
VANESSA: It means you're bringing good news for the entire world.
GABRIEL: I see. But as I understand it, I'm only talking to a few shepherds.
VANESSA: Yes, but the shepherds are only the beginning. They will be the first to see and witness the good news. And that's the next part of the speech.

**Gabriel:** "For unto you this day, in the city of David . . ." What city is that?

**Vanessa:** Bethlehem. They'll know where it is.

**Gabriel:** "A Savior is born. He is Christ the Lord." Who is that?

**Vanessa:** Who is that? Come on, Gabriel! You know who this is. It's Jesus!

**Gabriel:** You mean God's Son?

**Vanessa:** Yes.

**Gabriel:** What!? Born in Bethlehem? "Dressed in swaddling clothes and lying in a manger?"

**Vanessa:** Yes!

**Gabriel:** You must be joking! That's no place for the Son of God! He's the King of kings, the Prince of Peace. And He's going to be born and sleep in a stable full of animals?

**Vanessa:** Exactly.

**Gabriel:** That doesn't sound right to me.

**Vanessa:** Gabriel, where have you been? Didn't you know God is sending His son to die for their sins?

**Gabriel:** Die? Jesus is going to die?

**Vanessa:** Yes He is.

**Gabriel:** OK, that really sounds wrong to me.

**Vanessa:** But it's the only way to be reunited with His creation. This plan has been on the drawing board since the Garden of Eden closed. God was separated from His creation by sin, and the only way to reunite himself with His people is to die for their sins.

**Gabriel:** And that's why Jesus is being born?

**Vanessa:** Yes.

**Gabriel:** Wow! That is good news. That's great news!

**Vanessa:** Do you have your motivation now?

**Gabriel:** You bet I do! Quentin? Quentin! Hey, where did he go?

*[QUENTIN pops up.]*

**Quentin:** Sorry I'm late.

**Vanessa:** What kept you?

**Quentin:** Sorry, I had to switch arms. Poor guy got third-degree burns from the coffee.

*[A bandaged hand reaches up and shakes a fist at QUENTIN.]*

**Quentin:** Sorry. You ready?

**GABRIEL:** I sure am.
**QUENTIN:** OK, people. Let's do it right this time. Music!

*[Trumpets blast. QUENTIN and VANESSA exit.]*

**GABRIEL:** "Do not be afraid. I bring you good tidings of great joy that will be for all people. For unto you this day, in the city of David, a Savior is born. He is Christ the Lord. And this will be a sign to you. You will find him wrapped in swaddling clothes and lying in a manger."

*[VANESSA and QUENTIN pop up.]*

**ALL:** Glory to God in the highest! Peace on earth. Good will to men!

*[Blackout.]*

# Christmas While You Wait
by Susan Sundwall

**Summary:** Two days before Christmas, ANNIE and her brother CHUCK discover how meaningful it is to do something special for others while they wait for the big holiday.
**Characters:**
ANNIE—9-year-old girl
CHUCK—ANNIE'S 11-year-old brother
MOM—would work best if played by a teen girl
**Setting:** two chairs sit center stage in the living room; a Christmas tree is behind them stage left.
**Props:** two chairs, winter coats, bag of canned goods, sound device for car door slamming, small decorated tree.
**Costumes:** modern-day clothing

*CHUCK sits with his elbows on his knees, his chin in his hands, looking forward as though through a window.*

CHUCK: C'mon, c'mon!
ANNIE: *[enters stage right, sits next to CHUCK and looks out]* Bored?
CHUCK: It's two days to Christmas and I just know I'm getting new skis. But we need some snow. Look at that!
ANNIE: *[looks out again]* All I see is . . .
CHUCK: Dead grass and bare trees!
ANNIE: I don't know, Chuck. I kind of like the bare branches against the sky.
CHUCK: *[looks at her, disgusted]* Annie!
ANNIE: *[shrugs]* Sorry, there's nothing I can do to bring snow. I know something that might help though. Remember what the minister said last Sunday? It was all about waiting for Christmas and . . .
MOM: *[calls from off stage]* Annie . . . Chuck! *[rushes in, stage right, wearing winter coat and carrying a bag of canned goods]* There you are! I need some help you two.
ANNIE: What's going on Mom?
MOM: The van is full of bags for the food pantry and Mrs. Gibbons won't be able to help me with it.
CHUCK: *[grins and makes a muscle]* I guess I'm your man, Mom.
ANNIE: What do we have to do?

MOM: We'll take the food to the pantry, unload, and wait for people to pick it up.
CHUCK: All that? Oh man, that could take the rest of the afternoon!
ANNIE: *[snaps her fingers]* That's right. You had a lot of important things *[looking out the window for snow]* to do. Hey, Mom and I can handle it.
MOM: I'd really appreciate the help.
CHUCK: Yeah, OK.
ANNIE: *[makes a muscle, frowns and looks at CHUCK]* OK . . . you lift bags and I'll pass stuff out.
MOM: *[exits stage right and calls over her shoulder]* Let's go!
ANNIE: *[follows MOM]* Dashing through the snow . . . la, la, la.
CHUCK: *[gestures to ANNIE]* Hey, so what about waiting for Christmas . . . *[follows ANNIE out]*

*[Offstage, ANNIE and CHUCK put on winter coats. The stage is empty for about 20 seconds, and then a car door slams offstage.]*

CHUCK: *[enters stage right, removes coat and plops into chair]* Whew! I'm beat!
ANNIE: *[enters behind CHUCK looking bewildered, removes coat]* Wow, all those people.
CHUCK: It was somethin' huh?
ANNIE: That one little boy only had a sweater, no coat. And it's really cold out.
CHUCK: *[grins]* I threw in some extra snacks for him.
ANNIE: *[smiles at CHUCK]* I told his mom about the free turkey list at the church.
CHUCK: Hey, that might make their Christmas a little brighter! Nice going Sis!
ANNIE: Didn't it feel great helping out? The afternoon sure went fast.
CHUCK: Sure did. You know, I'm getting pretty hungry myself. I wonder what's for supper.
MOM: *[Enters stage right, brushing off her coat]* You both did such a good job today Dad and I are taking you to Angelo's for supper tonight.
ANNIE: *[claps]* Wahoo! I love Angelo's. I'll have extra cheese pizza and maybe canoli for dessert.
CHUCK: *[stares at MOM, points at her coat]* Is that . . .
MOM: *[brushes a few more flakes off her shoulder]* We'll have to get going though. It's starting to snow pretty hard.
CHUCK: *[throws both arms in the air]* I knew it! Snow!

MOM: Grab your coats. We'll be waiting in the car. *[exits stage right.]*
ANNIE: This is going to be the best Christmas! And we did just what the minister said.
CHUCK: *[turns to ANNIE]* Oh yeah, so what about waiting for Christmas?
ANNIE: *[gestures with hands outward]* It was real simple; do something for someone else while you wait.
CHUCK: *[laughs]* It sure beats waiting for snow; that's a real bore.
ANNIE: Waiting to eat, like those people at the pantry, is worse.
CHUCK: Yeah, I'm sure glad we could help. It was a good way to wait.
ANNIE: I hope we don't have to wait too long for our pizza. Oh, and Chuck?
CHUCK: Yeah.
ANNIE: What makes you so sure you're getting skis for Christmas?
CHUCK: I might have seen something in a closet . . .
ANNIE: *[gasps, lightly punches his arm and covers her mouth]* Oh, you didn't . . .
CHUCK: *[raises hands above his head]* Something about this long and . . .
ANNIE: You're so bad . . .

*[CHUCK and ANNIE exit stage right whispering and giggling about the skis. Blackout.]*

# From the Manger
by Dixie Phillips

**Summary:** A poetic rhythmic reading of the Christmas story.
**Characters:**
NARRATOR—would work best if played by a grandparent figure
DONKEY—male or female
MARY—mother of Jesus
JOSEPH—father of Jesus
INNKEEPER—male, should appear middle-aged
ANGELS—four are needed, can be male or female
SHEPHERDS—four are needed, can be male or female
WISEMEN—three are needed, all males
THE STAR—female
**Setting:** A stable setting stage right, NARRATOR opens at center stage. The children's recitations are done center stage and then after reciting their pieces they move to stage right and form a nativity scene for final scene.
**Props:** a stuffed lamb for SHEPHERD 1, WISEMEN should each have a wrapped gift to present to the baby Jesus, baby doll for baby Jesus, staffs for each SHEPHERD, rocking chair for NARRATOR, music for "Away in a Manger"
**Costumes:** Bible-times costumes, white robes for ANGELS, silver robe for THE STAR, modern-day dress for NARRATOR

*All lines are said in a rhythmic pattern. NARRATOR is sitting in a rocking chair at stage right to indicate he or she is a grandparent sharing the Christmas story.*

**NARRATOR:** The Christmas story never grows old. It's still the greatest story ever told. So you all sit back and enjoy the rhymes told by each girl and boy!

*[DONKEY, MARY & JOSEPH enter.]*

**DONKEY:** I am the donkey all fuzzy and brown. I carried Mary to that tiny town. HEEEE HAWWWW!
**MARY:** Joseph, we must stop right away. This baby will be born today.
**JOSEPH:** Look! There is an inn up ahead. Maybe they will have a room and bed.

*[JOSEPH pretends to knock on door.]*

**INNKEEPER:** We have no room for you on our farm. But I guess you can stay out back in the barn.

*[DONKEY, INNKEEPER, MARY, and JOSEPH take places in the stable stage right The four ANGELS enter flapping their wings as if flying down the center aisle.]*

**ANGEL 1:** I sang with all the angels who flew to earth to tell the shepherds of the Messiah's birth!
**ANGEL 2:** Jesus is born this day in tiny Bethlehem. A little town, but what a gem!
**ANGEL 3:** The littlest angels sang and tried not to squeak and through the stable's windows took a peek!
**ANGEL 4:** Angels here! Angels there! There were angels everywhere!

*[ANGELS take their place at the back of the stable as SHEPHERDS enter down the aisle.]*

**SHEPHERD 1:** *[carrying stuffed toy lamb]* I rejoiced the night my lost lamb was found. But when I saw the angels, I knew I was on holy ground.
**SHEPHERD 2:** My knees started shaking with sheer fright. *[shake knees]* When I saw all the angels in the sky that holy night!
**SHEPHERD 3:** We hurried to find where the babe did lay. He was sound asleep laying on manger filled with hay.
**SHEPHERD 4:** My eyes were shut; I was sound asleep. The angels singing woke me and all my sheep!

*[STAR enters down center aisle.]*

**STAR:** I am the star that shone brilliantly. But there is a light, Who shines brighter than me. Baby Jesus is the light sent from God above. He is Heaven's gift to us filled with love.

*[WISEMEN enter carrying gifts down center aisle.]*

**WISE MAN 1:** *[kneel by manger and present gift]* The star in the sky was quite a sight. It was bumpy riding a camel all night!

**WISE MAN 2:** *[kneel by manger and present gift]* Gold I bring. To the newborn king!

**WISE MAN 3:** *[kneel by manger and present gift]* My gift is frankincense! It's for the tiny prince!

*[The nativity scene should be set up at this point.]*

**ALL:** To *you [point to audience]* a child is born!

*Children sing "Away in a Manger."*

*[Blackout.]*

# Santa's Christmas Tree
by John Cosper

**Summary:** An all-star list of fairy-tale characters attend SANTA's Christmas party for food, fellowship, and SANTA's traditional telling of the birth of Christ.

**Characters:**
ANNOUNCER—any age, gives story's introduction
SANTA—jolly, old elf who makes toys
THE BIG BAD WOLF—hungry fairy-tale carnivore
CINDERELLA, SLEEPING BEAUTY, SNOW WHITE, RAPUNZEL—jilted fairy-tale princesses
LITTLE BO PEEP—a ditzy shepherd girl
RUMPELSTILTSKIN—a short guy and a con artist
BABE, PORKY, AND HAMMY—The Three Pigs
THE WICKED WITCH—Snow White's wicked stepmother
HANSEL AND GRETEL—candy-loving kids
THE CAMEL—a puppet who claims to be from a story
LITTLE RED RIDING HOOD, GOLDILOCKS—cute little fairytale girls
BO PEEP'S SHEEP—Sheep (nonspeaking roles)

**Setting:** the North Pole, elaborately decorated

**Props:** fairy-tale music, party favors, Christmas decorations, baby doll, a cross covered with a sheet, a stool, plate of cookies, glass of milk, buffet table with food, Christmas stockings (one with candy and one with coal)

**Costumes:** fairy tale costumes for all the characters, halo of tinsel for characters acting as angels, towels and headbands for Shepherd's headpieces for those acting as Shepherds, Mary, and Joseph

*Lights Out. Fairy-tale music plays to open scene.*

**ANNOUNCER:** Once upon a time, in a faraway land of fairy tales, Santa hosted a Christmas party. Everyone came from miles around for this night of celebration to hear Santa tell the Christmas story and to witness the unveiling of the Christmas tree.

*[Lights up. The stage is set for a party. A cross is standing at upstage center, covered by a sheet. The sheet should be set over the cross to make it look like a Christmas tree underneath. The CAMEL is sitting behind a table stage left with HANSEL and GRETEL. A buffet table is set up stage right, and*

Bo Peep's Sheep *are gathered around it eating.* Rumpelstiltskin *stands behind them, trying to get at the buffet.* Snow White, *the* Witch, *and* The Three Pigs *are down stage right.* Bo Peep *is down stage left, pouting. The other characters mingle at center stage.]*

**Babe:** Mmmm! This is delicious. Snow White, you gotta have some of this fruitcake!
**Snow:** Fruitcake? Do you know how much fat is in that?
**Babe:** I don't care about fat grams! I'm a pig!
**Rumpel:** *[yells]* Hey, Peep! Peep, your sheep are hogging the buffet! Come on, get 'em out of my way!
**Babe:** Just leave it to me! *["baaa!" and move away from the buffet.]*
**Rumpel:** Thanks, Babe.
**Babe:** Don't mention it.

*[The* Wicked Witch *and* The Big Bad Wolf *walk to down stage left and take their place. The* Wolf *and the* Witch *carry Christmas stockings.]*

**Wolf:** Hey, Queenie!
**Witch:** Hey, Big Bad. What did you get from Santa?
**Wolf:** Same as always. A stocking full of coal!
**Witch:** Loser! I got candy!
**Wolf:** Candy? How? Did you go good?
**Witch:** Goodness no, honey. I just switched stockings with Gretel!
**Wolf:** It's good to be bad!

*[The* Wolf *and the* Witch *step back to center stage so* Hansel *and* Gretel *are seen.]*

**Camel:** Wowee. I can't believe this! You're really Hansel and Gretel! This is truly an honor.
**Gretel:** So . . . which story are you in?
**Hansel:** Yeah. I've never heard any stories about a camel.
**Camel:** Well, you know, I was in . . . that one.
**Hansel:** Which one?
**Camel:** You know. The one with the camel!
**Gretel:** There are no fairy tales about camels!
**Camel:** Yes there are! I was in it!

[CINDERELLA, SNOW WHITE, RAPUNZEL, and SLEEPING BEAUTY *walk to down stage left in front of* HANSEL, GRETEL, *and the* CAMEL.]

SNOW: Forget Prince Charming, I know just the guy for you. He's a little short, but he's a very sweet guy.
BEAUTY: Are you trying to set me up with a dwarf? What could we possibly have in *[yawn]* common?
SNOW: More than you know!
BEAUTY: Yeah? What's his name?
SNOW: Sleepy.
CAMEL: I got it! The Musicians of Bremen!
GRETEL: There were no camels in The Musicians of Bremen.
CAMEL: How the Camel Got His Hump! That's got camel in the title!
GRETEL: Those stories don't count! What fairy tale were you in?

[SANTA *enters.*]

CAMEL: Hey look! It's Santa!

[ALL, *except the* CAMEL, *run to surround* SANTA.]

SANTA: Ho, ho, ho! Merry Christmas everyone!
ALL: Merry Christmas, Santa.
SANTA: Hey, can I ask a question, does this suit make me look fat?

[ALL *laugh at* SANTA's *joke.*]

RED: Santa, I wanna hear the Christmas story now!
ALL: Yeah! Now! We wanna hear it now! Please?
SANTA: I don't know. Santa's pretty tired. I don't know if I can tell it without—

[CINDERELLA *runs up with cookies and a glass of milk.*]

CINDY: Milk and cookies?
SANTA: That's my girl! Thank you, Cinderella!

[RUMPELSTILTSKIN *sets a stool next to* SANTA. SANTA *puts the cookies and milk on the stool. He eats one cookie and drinks some milk. The rest of the cast sits on the stage behind* SANTA *in a semicircle.* SANTA *faces the audience as he begins.*]

Santa's Christmas Tree

**Santa:** Long ago, in a far away land, there lived a man named Joseph and a girl named Mary.

*[Snow White and Rumpelstiltskin stand up.]*

**Santa:** Mary and Joseph were engaged, but before they were married, Mary was visited by an angel who said . . .

*[Cinderella stands up as the angel.]*

**Cindy:** Do not be afraid, for you have found favor in the eyes of God. You will give birth to a son. He will be called the Son of the Most High, and His kingdom will never end.
**Santa:** Soon after the angel appeared to Mary, the same angel appeared to Joseph.
**Cindy:** Joseph, do not be afraid to take Mary as your wife. The child that is inside of her is from the Holy Spirit, and you shall give Him the name Jesus.
**Santa:** So Joseph took Mary as his wife, just like the angel told him. When the time came for the baby to be born, Joseph and Mary were in Joseph's hometown of Bethlehem. All the inns were full, so baby Jesus was born in a stable.

*[Red Riding Hood hands Snow White a doll to be the baby. Snow White and Rumpelstiltskin kneel down center stage with the baby.]*

**Santa:** He spent that first night lying in a manger, surrounded by pigs, sheep, and even a camel.

*[The Three Little Pigs and Sheep gather around Snow White and Rumpelstiltskin.]*

**Camel:** See, I told you I was in this story!
**Santa:** On that same night, a group of shepherds were watching their flocks.

*[Bo Peep, Red Riding Hood, and Golidilocks (the Shepherds) stand up at stage left.]*

**Santa:** Suddenly, the angel of the Lord appeared to them, saying . . .

**Cindy:** Fear not, I bring you good news for all people. Today in the city of Bethlehem, a Savior has been born, who is Christ the Lord.

*[Sleeping Beauty, the Witch, Rapunzel, and Gretel [Angels] stand up with Cinderella.]*

**Santa:** Suddenly a host of angels appeared, singing praises to God. The shepherds ran into Bethlehem and found everything just as the angel had told them.

*[The shepherds kneel around Snow White, Rumpelstiltskin, and the animals. The angels begin singing "O Come All Ye Faithful" softly. The Wolf, the Prince, and Hansel stand up and walk into the scene as the three Magi.]*

**Santa:** Some time later, Wise Men from the east visited the new born king. They followed a star to Bethlehem, bringing Jesus gifts of gold and spices fit for a king.

*[Gretel and Sleeping Beauty walk backstage to the cross, standing on either side of it.]*

**Santa:** But great as those gifts were, the greatest present given that night was the tiny baby in the manger. As a child he was only the son of a carpenter. As a man, He became known as the Son of God. That is why, on this cold December night, we remember the baby. We remember the angels who sang. We remember the gifts of the Wise Men. And if we are truly wise, we remember the gift this tiny baby would one day give on another tree, the greatest gift of all.

*[Gretel and Sleeping Beauty rip off the sheet, revealing the cross. The angels sing the end of the verse, then lights out. Blackout.]*

# Silent Night Surprise
by Brett Parker

**Summary**: The NORTH STAR is feeling down and angry because he doesn't know why God is making him shine over Bethlehem.
**Characters**:
THE NORTH STAR—male or female
**Setting**: in the sky above Bethlehem
**Props**: none
**Costumes**: a silver robe or cardboard star cutout

*Enters the stage from side and slowly meanders around. Paces back and forth on stage, as if he is pouting.*

**NORTH STAR:** Oh. *[noticing crowd]* I didn't see you there. Hello. *[puts head back down to pout some more. He walks to the center of the stage and sits down with his legs folded Indian style and rest his head on his hands.]* I'm the North Star. And I . . . am . . . so . . . *[yawns]* B-O-R-E-D, bored. Just take a look around. *[looks around]* Do you know where this is? Do you have any idea where we are? *[gives audience a second to answer]* That's right, we're in Bethlehem. I'm stuck here in boring, ole' Bethlehem. How did I get here you might ask? *[stands up]* Well let me tell you! *[becoming upset]*

A couple years ago, God told me that He had a special job for me. He told me that I was going to get to shine over a *very* important city and that I would get to show people the way to a *very* special person. So where did God put me? Right here in plain, dull Bethlehem. There's nothing to do here! It's so boring! Why couldn't God send me to somewhere cool, like Rome? *[looking off dreamily]* Or maybe Athens? Yeah! Or what about Jerusalem?! Or even Miami Beach! All of those would have been more exciting than *Bethlehem*!

All I do is sit around all day and night and shine. And for what? Where is this SPECIAL person I'm supposed to be showing the way to for other? Who is he? *[begins to pace and stomp around again.]* Some important city this is. *[mumbling and complaining to himself]* Bethlehem. More like Boring-hem! *[notices something off in the distance]* Hmm.

That's strange. Looks like there's a large group of people walking toward the city. *[shakes his head]* Who would come to Bethlehem at this time of night? *[shrugs it off]* Oh well, must be some folks who are coming from Jerusalem and need a place to stop and rest for the night. *[looks more closely]* Wait a second. They are all riding on camels. And . . . what's that they're wearing? *[surprised]* I can't believe it! They're dressed like kings!

What in the world would kings be doing in Bethlehem?! And look at all the things they have with them! Wow! They have some gold and other fine metals! Is that expensive perfumes I smell?! *[a thought pops into his mind]* Maybe one of these kings or Wise Men is the special person that I'm supposed to shine on! *[he begins to move around excitedly for the first time]* Oh boy! I wonder who this king is? I wonder where he is from? Is he coming to rule over Bethlehem? Maybe even the whole nation of Israel?! This is so exciting! *[points down as if he is looking over the city]*

Look at that! Look at them walk through the streets. Oh! Do you see all the people looking out of their houses? I bet they're wondering what's going on! *[laughs]* Ha, ha! If only they knew what I do. Where are they going now? It looks like they are stopping in front of Joseph's and Mary's house. Why would kings be stopping at *their* house? Isn't Joseph just a carpenter?

Hey look! They're getting off their camels! *[watches intensely]* One of the Wise Men is knocking at the door. *[gasps]* Joseph is letting them come inside! Bow, Joseph! Bow!! He is a king! You have to bow! What could those kings possibly want with people like Joseph and Mary? *[taps foot on floor while he is deep in thought. he looks down again and is shocked at what he finds]* Hey! Is that baby Jesus? Why is Mary bringing baby Jesus to all those kings? What are they doing now? *[jumps back in astonishment and points down below him]*

They're giving all of those beautiful gifts to baby Jesus! Why are they giving them to Jesus? Shouldn't they be giving those gifts to someone more important? They should be giving those to the governor of the city or one of the priests that works in the synagogue. Jesus is just an ordinary person! *[gasps again]*

Silent Night Surprise

You'll never believe what they're doing now! All of the kings and Wise Men are . . . *bowing* to baby Jesus. Why would kings bow to a little baby? Shouldn't it be the other way around? Wait! *[puts finger over mouth to shush audience]* Shhh! One of them is saying something! He's praising baby Jesus! He's calling him the Messiah. He said that *Jesus* was a king! He called him the king of the *world*! He said that Jesus is . . . the Son of God? So is that what God was talking about when He told me that I would lead people to a special person? Was Jesus this special person all along? *[a joyful expression comes on his face]* Wow!

I got to lead people to God's Son, the one and only Messiah that everyone has been waiting for! I guess God did know what He was talking about when He gave me a job to do! From now on I'm going to do every job that God gives me with a cheerful attitude! Thanks God! I got to show people the way to Jesus, the king of the world! *[points to audience]* And don't forget . . . you can too! *[Exits. Blackout.]*

# A Donkey's Story
by Alyce Pickett

**Summary:** In a rhythmic and poetic monologue, the donkey that Joseph and Mary rode into Bethlehem tells his side of the story of Christ's birth.
**Character:**
DONKEY—male or female
**Setting:** outside the stable where Christ was born
**Costume:** donkey outfit

*Lights up on* DONKEY.

DONKEY: If I could talk, I'd tell you a story. Every word is true, even though it comes from me, Joseph's little brown donkey.

My master's wife rode one day on my back a long, long way. Up and down each rocky hill I plodded on the way until we reached the town of Bethlehem as day's light was growing dim.

I was as tired as could be and when he came again, we three went to a stable, nice and quiet and they stayed there with me that night. I got next to the wall and lay after eating my fill of hay.

Soon I slept . . . heard nothing more 'til shepherd men were at the door. From sheepfold they had come to bring praises to a Christ child king.

*What is this?* I stood to see in the manger a new baby. *Is that a King?* I wondered then, *Will He rule in the lives of men? How could I praise this baby King?* I couldn't shout, I couldn't sing.

I was very happy that He shared the stable there with me. I only want to let you know what happened that night long ago, and ask a favor now of you, Praise the Christ child for me too.

*[Blackout.]*

# Prayer Mail
by Paula Reed

**Summary:** What would happen if God treated our prayers in the same way we handle communication with each other. What if He installed voice mail?

**Characters:**
ANGEL 1—supervisor type, helping set the scene
ANGEL 2—receptionist, new at the job, polite but detached
PERSON PRAYING—trying to have her quiet time with God, becomes confused and frustrated

**Props:** desk, chair, small table, Bible, thick binder, headphones, phone.

**Setting**: one side of the stage is Heaven and the other side should look like a bedroom

**Costumes:** white robes for ANGEL 1 and ANGEL 2, modern-day clothing for PERSON PRAYING

*ANGEL 1 is behind ANGEL 2 helping her get everything arranged. [Option: above the desk could be golden arches with a sign that says: Over 20 Billion Served Daily.] Thick manual is placed before ANGEL 2, she is also arranging her headphones, pen and paper, etc. To the other side of the stage is a chair with small table beside it with Bible and phone on the table.*

ANGEL 1: All set?

ANGEL 2: I think so.

ANGEL 1: Heavenly. Just remember you have your manual here in front of you. It should cover just about any request.

ANGEL 2: I'm ready. But may I ask just exactly why He decided to install prayer mail?

ANGEL 1: Well, I've been told there was a meeting with all department heads and the archangel in charge of the prayer department suggested we try this new system. Prayer is becoming quite a challenge—yesterday we logged in over 20 billion requests! And with the approaching Christmas season those prayer requests will double or even triple.

ANGEL 2: Wow! Why is that?

ANGEL 1: EVERYONE gets on the prayer wagon during Christmas. Children pray that God will deliver, in case Santa doesn't, and adults pray they can pay for the delivery—if you know what I mean.

ANGEL 2: I do. But don't you think this voice mail idea might seem a bit . . . impersonal to humans?

ANGEL 1: Oh, heavens no! They're used to this sort of thing—it's how they communicate. Now, remember, be pleasant but impersonal and try not to get too attached to the caller.
ANGEL 2: OK. Thanks for all your help.
ANGEL 1: Bye, Gabriella. And have a heavenly day.

[ANGEL 1 exits. PERSON PRAYING comes to center stage and begins by getting on her knees, next to the chair.]

PERSON: Good morning, Lord. I look forward to this quiet time with you and . . .
ANGEL 1: [interrupts] Thank you for calling the prayer offices of the Lord Jehovah. This call may be monitored for training purposes. Please hold.
PERSON: [clearly startled] Whoa! What in the world was that? I knew I shouldn't have had those Christmas cookies right before I went to bed. [shakes head as if to clear it] I think maybe I'll try reading some Scripture first. [gets up and sits in chair, picks up Bible, bows head] Lord, please help me to understand what I'm about to . . .
ANGEL 1: [interrupting again] Thank you for holding. Please select one of the following options . . .
PERSON: [interrupts and nearly drops Bible at the sound of the voice] Wait a minute! I don't understand this!
ANGEL 1: I'm sorry but, "I don't understand this" is not a valid response. Please pick up your phone and select one of the following options: [PERSON, in frustration, picks up phone on table and listens while ANGEL 1 continues.] For praise and thanksgiving, press 1. For personal requests, press 2. For other requests, press 3. For confessions, you may press numbers 4 through 7. For wisdom and understanding, press 8. To dictate your Christmas wish list, press 9. For all other prayers, please stay on the line and one of our prayer service ANGELs will assist you momentarily. Please keep in mind that your prayer will be handled in the order it was received. Approximate waiting time at this point is 3 hours and 20 minutes. To listen to these options again, please press the pound key now.
PERSON: I can't believe I'm doing this! [presses button in frustration]
ANGEL 1: You have reached the praise and thanksgiving department. Your praise is very important to us. However, to expedite your praise, please record your message after the beep. When you are finished you may hang up or press # for further options.

Prayer Mail

**Person:** This is crazy!

**Angel 1:** I'm sorry but, "this is crazy" is not a valid praise response. Please try again.

**Person:** *[flustered]* OK, OK. *[Begins to pray while on the phone]* Lord, You are an awesome God and I thank You for all that You have done for me.

**Angel 1:** Thank you, and be assured that your praise is appreciated. To return to the main menu, press the pound key now.

**Person:** *[pushing button and completely bewildered]* I just don't understand any of this!

**Angel 1:** For wisdom and understanding, press 8 now.

**Person:** *[pressing buttons]* I'm pressing! I'm pressing!

**Angel 2:** You have reached the wisdom and understanding department. Please listen carefully to the following options: For help in parenting, press 1 now. Due to the high volume of callers please be advised the wait time could be several hours. However, while on hold you have the option of listening to King David's Music of Psalms. For help on the Old Testament, press 2 to reach Moses now and for help on the New Testament, press 3 to reach Paul now. For wisdom on how to deal with all the relatives during Christmas, please hang up and try again. For knowledge about the final destination of a departed loved one, please enter their Social Security number now. For puzzling questions related to the age of the earth, dinosaurs, the location of Noah's ark or other biblical mysteries, please write them down and bring them with you when you arrive.

**Person:** *[really frustrated now]* Look, I just want to talk to God, not some impersonal machine! *[collects herself]* God, I'm sorry, is this my punishment for the way I acted yesterday when I received Aunt Geraldine's fruitcake and threw it at . . .

**Angel 1:** *[interrupts]* To reach the confession department press 4 now.

**Person:** *[angrily pushes button]* Fine!

**Angel 2:** You have reached the Department of Confessions and Corrections. We realize this call was probably difficult for you to make . . .

**Person:** *[interrupting]* You can say that again!

**Angel 2:** We realize this call was probably difficult for you to make, therefore, angels are standing by ready to take your confession. To expedite the high volume of confessions we receive, especially during Christmas, please listen carefully. On a scale of 1-10 with 10 being the most serious offense, please determine the severity of your sin and then select one of the following options: For sins 1-3, press 5 to reach an angel now, for sins 4-6, press 6 to speak directly to Michael or Gabriel, for sins 7-9, press 7 for a conference call with a legion of angels, and if your sin has reached the magnitude of #10, please remain on the line and you will be connected with someone from Satan's Social Services who is eagerly awaiting your call.

PERSON: How am I supposed to know how to rate my sin? Isn't that your department?

ANGEL 2: To find out if you've been naughty or nice, the newly formed Scale of Sin Department will be happy to assist you. However, please be advised that their office is temporarily closed due to the holiday season. They would like to wish everyone a very Merry Christmas.

PERSON: *[screams out of frustration]* Merry Christmas? This isn't merry; this is scary! I need help right now—please!

ANGEL 1: You have reached the personal request department. Once again, due to the extremely high volume of requests, please limit your request to 1 major cry for help. If your cry for help is of an urgent nature, please visit your nearest chapel now for immediate assistance.

PERSON: *[totally distraught]* I'm begging you—please, please put me through to the *living* God—now!

ANGEL 1: Thank you. I'll connect you now.

PERSON: *[breathes a sigh of relief]* Thank God!

ANGEL 2: *[begins to connect PERSON but stops after hearing her response]* You have reached the praise and thanksgiving department.

PERSON: *[screams in frustration and slams the phone down]* This can't be happening! *[tries to collect herself here]* OK, that couldn't be real—I must have been having some kind of nightmare or something. I'm just going to start all over again–just breathe, relax, and go to God in prayer. *[bows head]* Dear Lord, I just want to spend some time with you this . . .

ANGEL 2: *[interrupts]* I'm sorry. Our records indicate you have already called once today. Please hang up and try again tomorrow. Our prayer offices open at 9:00 AM, earth time. Thank you for calling and have a Merry Christmas.

PERSON: That's it! I'm going to go eat all the cookies!

*[Blackout.]*

# The Christmas Toys
by John Cosper

**Summary:** A story about two toys that want to know who is the greatest Christmas gift of all.
**Characters:**
NARRATOR—lines could be said from offstage
CAPTAIN JOHNNY JUMPKICK—any age male, dressed as little boy's action figure
BONNIE BRIGHT-EYES—any age female, dressed as a little girl's doll
SANTA CLAUS
MARY
JOSEPH
**Setting:** *[by scene]*
Underneath a Christmas tree—wrapped presents, gifts propped up, large tree trunk at center [if possible]
Bethlehem—manger scene
**Props:** Christmas tree, a big, red ball, wrapped Christmas packages, a manger, baby doll for the baby Jesus
**Costumes:** space suit, little girl dress, Santa suit, Bible-times costumes
**Director's Notes:** The flow of the play has rhythmic pattern like a poem so the exchanges between characters should flow as such to complete the rhymes.

## Scene 1: Underneath the Christmas Tree

*JOHNNY and BONNIE are on stage sleeping beside a big red ball. NARRATOR should be off to the side of the stage [or offstage] for all of his lines.*

**NARRATOR:** Once upon a snowy eve, the Christmas lights were gleaming
From all around a Christmas tree to three small toys still sleeping.
A Captain Johnny Jumpkick toy slept by a big, red ball.
The third toy was the first awake—a Bonnie Bright-eyes doll.
**BONNIE:** It's Christmas Eve! Wake up! Wake up!
**NARRATOR:** She shouted with a grin.
**JOHNNY:** Aw knock it off,
**NARRATOR:** Johnny snapped back.
**JOHNNY:** I'm trying to sleep in.
**BONNIE:** The time has come. It's finally here! And soon one lucky girl
Will wake and find me sitting here—the best gift in the world.

**Johnny:** I don't think so,
**Narrator:** Said Johnny Jumpkick hopping to his feet.
**Johnny:** No silly doll can do the things that make this hero neat!
**Bonnie:** I'm not,
**Narrator:** She huffed,
**Bonnie:** A silly doll, and if you're really bright,
  You'd see in every way that I'm a little girl's delight!
  I'm a limited edition and they call me Bonnie Bright-Eyes.
  I'm the only doll you'll ever see who blinks and winks and cries.
  The girls all love my pretty dress and hair that they can comb.
  The only thing I really need is somewhere to call home.
**Narrator:** She ended with a bow and followed with a graceful twirl.
  Then Johnny said,
**Johnny:** You've much to learn, you silly, silly girl!
  I'm Captain Johnny Jumpkick and as any one can see,
  I'm easily a cooler toy than you will ever be!
  I use my ninja powers to fight green monsters from space
  And nobody has ever beat my spaceship in a race!
**Narrator:** The two stared at each other while the ball made not a peep,
  Because everybody knows a big, red ball cannot speak.
  Then Bonnie said,
**Bonnie:** We're wasting time by getting in a fight.
  There's only one way we can know which one of us is right.
  We have to go and ask the man whose beard grows white and thick.
**Narrator:** Then Johnny said,
**Johnny:** You're right! We'll have to ask dear old St. Nick!
**Narrator:** And even as he said that name, they heard a strange new sound
  As down the chimney Santa dropped and landed on the ground.

[SANTA *enters.*]

**Bonnie** and **Johnny:** Good, Santa!
**Narrator:** Cried the two small toys,
**Bonnie:** Please share with us your wisdom,
**Johnny:** And tell us who's the greatest gift throughout the Christmas kingdom!
**Narrator:** The jolly, fat man laughed as only Santa Claus can do,
  And said,
**Santa:** I think I know just how to help the two of you.

The Christmas Toys

We'll have to take a journey to a land that's far away
To show you why we celebrate with gifts on Christmas Day.
We're going back in time, where the two of you will see
A gift that came one Christmas Day that changed all history.

## Scene 2: Bethlehem

*The toys exit with SANTA. As the NARRATOR speaks, MARY and JOSEPH enter with the baby Jesus and walk to the side of stage that is decorated like Bethlehem. JOHNNY, BONNIE, and SANTA then reenter.*

**NARRATOR:** The toys agreed and with a wink were quickly swept away
   And found themselves flying away in Santa's reindeer sleigh.
   They traveled far into the night 'til both were half asleep,
   Then softly were awakened by the gentle baa of sheep.
   The sleigh had landed in a barn of animals and hay
   And a couple near a manger where a tiny baby lay.
   Bonnie looked and Johnny looked to find the special toy,
   The greatest gift that anyone could give a girl or boy.
   But everywhere the toys would look, no packages were found,
   So Bonnie asked St. Nick,
**BONNIE:** Where can this greatest gift be found?
**JOHNNY:** What is it, Santa?
**NARRATOR:** Johnny asked,
**JOHNNY:** A teddy bear or ball?
   Where is this special toy you call the greatest gift of all?
**SANTA:** The greatest gift,
**NARRATOR:** Santa began,
**SANTA:** Is not a ball or doll,
   In fact the Christmas present here is not a toy at all!
   Look at the child who's sleeping softly in His mother's arms,
   The child who's snuggled tightly in old rags to keep Him warm.
   Look in the eyes of that small child and surely you will find
   It's Jesus Christ, the King of kings and Savior of mankind!
**NARRATOR:** Bonnie was shocked.
**BONNIE:** This can't be right, this baby that we've found,
   How can a baby be the greatest gift of all?
**NARRATOR:** She frowned.
   Then Santa smiled and said,
**SANTA:** This gift is more than just a toy.

It's God the Father's perfect gift of love and peace and joy.
God sent his only son to earth to die upon a cross.
He came to set His people free and save a world that's lost.
He came to give the world new life by giving Hhis away,
And that's the very reason we give gifts on Christmas Day.

**NARRATOR:** Then Captain Johnny Jumpkick and the Bonnie Bright-Eyes doll
Approached the newborn King sleeping in the stable stall.
They kneeled with Santa by the child amid the hay and grass
And there inside the stable found the greatest gift at last!

*[Blackout.]*

# Turkey Trouble
by Brett Parker

**Summary**: A fat, happy-go-lucky Timmy the Turkey wakes up to what he thinks is just another average day but soon discovers that it is the day before Thanksgiving . . . and he's on the menu!
**Characters**:
TIMMY THE TURKEY—male, costume should be stuffed so he appears very round
**Setting**: the backyard of a farmhouse
**Props**: alarm clock, calendar
**Costumes**: turkey suit, possibly brown sweat suit and a beak

*TIMMY is sound asleep on the ground. He is snoring loudly! He is suddenly awakened by his alarm clock. He jolts and quickly turns it off.*

**TIMMY:** Morning already?! *[stretches his arms while he is still sitting in bed]* I was sleeping so well, what a great night's sleep! *[quickly stands up]* Good morning, world! *[looks around]* What a beautiful, autumn day!

Hi everyone, I'm Timmy the Turkey, and I just love mornings in the fall! You see, I live on Farmer John's place, and there is nothing like morning time here on the farm! The roosters crowing, the horses eating their morning grain, the pretty leaves falling off the trees, and *[points in excitement]* OH! And the pigs are already wallowing in the mud! They are so funny! Yes folks, I have a good life.

Well, let's see . . . what am I going to do today? Hmm . . . ? *[looks up in thought]* Take a walk down by the pond? *[shakes head]* Nah, I did that yesterday. Chase Farmer John's wife around and gobble really loud? *[makes a loud gobble sound. Laughs aloud]* Oh, that would be so fun! Perhaps I could do that later. Maybe I could go visit with the cows this morning. I bet they'd love to chat! *[looks off in the distance]* Looks like they are eating right now. I wouldn't want to disturb them. Hey! Is that Farmer John? *[puts hand over eyes as if to shield the sun to look far in the distance]* What is he doing out in the field today? Looks like he has a basket there. And it's full of delicious food! *[rubs stomach hungrily]* Corn, . . . tomatoes, . . . carrots . . . *[in disgust]* squash?! Gross! Ok, well almost everything looks good to eat.

Oh, and there is Farmer John's son. Ahh, it looks like he is carrying a huge pumpkin! Wow! What could they be gathering all this food for? Maybe they're planning a great, big feast! Boy, oh boy! *[licks his lips]* I love feasts! I wonder what they are celebrating. Is it someone's birthday? Let's check the ole' calendar here!

*[Grabs calendar. Gleefully hums or whistles a tune while he is flipping through the pages of calendar.]*

Wednesday, November *[pauses]* Hey, that means that tomorrow is Thanksgiving Day! Yippee! *[jumps in excitement]* What a great day! All the good food! So that's what they are gathering all the food for! I can't wait! All that delicious food. Oh, I wonder what Farmer John's wife will be cooking. *[sniffs the air]* Man! I can already smell those wonderful smells! The pumpkin pie, the cranberry sauce, the dressing, the gravy, the turkey, the—*[realizes what he just said]* Oh no! *[drops the calendar and lets out a long serious of gobble sounds]*

Turkey?! I'm a turkey! What am I going to do?! They are going to eat me! Those mongrels! *[raises fist angrily in the air]* I know what I'll do! I'm going to exercise! That's it! Nobody wants a skinny turkey! *[starts to run in place]* That's it, Timmy! Keep jogging! *[quickly gets tired and begins panting hard]* Oh who am I kidding? This will never work! I knew I shouldn't have snuck into the chicken coop and eaten all that chicken feed! Oh, what to do? *[to himself]*

Ok, Timmy, hold on one second. Just calm down. *[takes a deep breath]* Maybe they won't eat me. That's right, surely they wouldn't eat me. Farmer John and I are good friends. I'll just go to Farmer John and have a talk with him. Yeah, that's what I'll do. I'll just talk with Farmer John and explain to him that he and his family can have Thanksgiving without a turkey. *[thinks for a moment]*

Well, I mean, I *guess* they could enjoy a good Thanksgiving meal without turkey, right? *[sighs]* I know, I know. It's just not Thanksgiving without a turkey. It wouldn't be fair of me to ask Farmer John and his family not to celebrate the things that they are thankful for on Thanksgiving Day. Farmer John has given me everything that I have, and I guess it's time that I stopped thinking of myself and started doing things for others. After all, that's what Jesus did, isn't it?

Turkey Trouble

Jesus sacrificed himself when he went to the cross to die for our sins. He wasn't thinking of himself, but instead He was thinking of everybody here. *[points to audience]* And He was thinking of me too. *[begins to cheer up]* Well you know what? I'm going to do what Jesus did! I'm going to start thinking of others before myself. I'm thankful for my life and what I have been blessed with! And to show my thanks, I'm going to be the best Thanksgiving Day turkey that Farmer John and his family ever tasted! *[looks at himself]*

Oh, wow! I'm looking thin! If Farmer John is going to have me for his Thanksgiving meal, I had better start fattening up! Hey chickens! *[yells off to the side]* Don't eat all your food yet! I need to get fat quick! *[exits off the side of stage. Blackout.]*

# The Turkey Thanksgiving
by John Cosper

**Summary:** A little girl meets a group of turkeys celebrating their own Thanksgiving holiday.
**Characters:**
Missi—little girl
Ralph, Arnold, Lisa, Joanie—turkeys
**Setting:** the woods with a table with chairs
**Props:** food for Thanksgiving minus the turkey
**Costumes:** little girl clothes for Missi; turkey costumes for the Turkeys

*Some large rocks or trees are in the background, with the Turkeys hiding behind them. At center is a long table, all set with veggies and pies, as if for a feast. Missi skips on stage, and stops when she sees the table.*

**Missi:** Hey! What's this table doing here? Wow, look at all the food! Sweet potatoes, green beans, and cranberries!

*[Ralph looks up from behind a tree. Joanie pulls him back.]*

**Missi:** It almost looks like a Thanksgiving dinner. Maybe it was set by wood nymphs! Or elves! Or fairies! Wow, how cool would that be? They even have my favorite pecan pie!

*[Lisa looks out.]*

**Lisa:** That's my pie!

*[Arnold pulls Lisa back before Missi sees her.]*

**Missi:** Everything's here, but where's the turkey?

*[Ralph looks out.]*

**Ralph:** Duh!

*[Joanne pulls Ralph back into hiding. Missi turns to look.]*

**Missi:** Hello? Is someone here? Don't be afraid! I won't hurt you!

[ARNOLD *steps out.*]

ARNOLD: Yeah, sure you won't!

[JOANIE *jumps out.*]

JOANIE: What are you doing? Now she's gonna eat us!
ARNOLD: Please! She doesn't have a gun or a carving knife, and I don't see any ovens.

[RALPH *looks out.*]

RALPH: You mean she's harmless?
ARNOLD: Harmless as a human kid can be.
MISSI: Oh my goodness! I've never seen talking turkeys!
RALPH: You've obviously never been to Washington DC!

[TURKEYS *come out, walking toward* MISSI *and the table.*]

MISSI: Is this your meal?
LISA: That's right, kid. It's the day after the fourth Friday in November. And that means it's Turkey Thanksgiving.
MISSI: Turkey Thanksgiving?
LISA: You betcha!
JOANIE: Fine, Lisa, let's just tell the whole world.
LISA: Hey, she found us fair and square. She might as well know. Besides, who would believe a bunch of turkeys eating Thanksgiving dinner?
MISSI: Not me! I thought turkeys hated Thanksgiving!
ARNOLD: Are you kidding? Thanksgiving is very big with us turkeys!
MISSI: It is?
ARNOLD: Oh yeah!
MISSI: How come?
LISA: Well, for one thing, we turkeys are very spiritual. We love the Lord, and we are very thankful for the blessings He gives us.
MISSI: Is that so?
RALPH: And the other big reason . . . those of us who lived through yesterday have a lot to be thankful for!
MISSI: I guess that's true.
JOANIE: You see, kid, we turkeys understand something you humans need to learn. No matter what life brings, God is good, and we have a lot to

be thankful for. Like this year, I am thankful that I have three new nieces and two new nephews in my family.

**Arnold:** And I am thankful for the beautiful weather we saw this fall.

**Lisa:** I'm thankful for the campers that left their library books. I love reading!

**Ralph:** I'm thankful for vegetarians. And vegans. And people who prefer ham or lamb or even pasta on Thanksgiving.

**Arnold:** I think we're all thankful for that.

**Missi:** This is such a great surprise! It's just like how we celebrate at my house: everyone eating together and remembering how good God is.

**Arnold:** Say, kid, would you like to join us?

**Missi:** Why, I think that would be lovely!

**Lisa:** Wait! Before she sits down, she has to do it.

**Missi:** Do what?

**Joanie:** Tell us what you're thankful for.

**Missi:** Oh that's easy!

**Ralph:** So go for it!

**Missi:** I'm thankful for my mom and dad and baby brother. I'm thankful for Jesus. And, I'm thankful that it's a month to the best holiday of the year, Christmas!

*[Turkeys look at each other in alarm.]*

**Lisa:** Wait! Did you say . . . CHRISTMAS?

**Arnold:** Run for the hills!

*[Turkeys gobble and run away. Blackout.]*

# Thankful for Pie
by Susan Sundwall

**Summary:** While ANNIE and her brother CHUCK are thinking of things they're thankful for, GRANDPA is suddenly in trouble, but the reason turns out to be a big surprise for everyone.

**Characters:**
CHUCK—11 year-old boy
ANNIE—his 9 year-old sister
GRANDMA WHITE—best if played by teen or adult
MOM—best if played by teen or adult
GRANDPA WHITE—best if played by teen or adult

**Setting:** Thanksgiving Day in the living room of ANNIE and CHUCK's home.

**Set:** two chairs covered with a throw to look like a couch sit center stage

**Props:** two chairs, throw, pizza box, pie plate covered with foil for pumpkin pie

**Costumes:** modern-day clothing

*CHUCK enters stage left, sniffs the air.*

**CHUCK:** Ah, the wonderful smell of roasting turkey! *[Sits on couch and puts feet up.]*

*[ANNIE enters stage right, sniffs the air and makes a face.]*

**ANNIE:** Ooh! I hate that smell.
**CHUCK:** You can't possibly mean the turkey.
**ANNIE:** Oh, yes, I can. Why can't we have pizza for Thanksgiving?
**CHUCK:** *[sits up, shocked]* But—turkey's a tradition that goes back even before Dad was born!
**ANNIE:** *[hands on hips]* Then maybe he's ready for a change!
**CHUCK:** You'd never talk Dad out of turkey and stuffing.
**ANNIE:** Well, I'd be a lot more thankful if we could have pizza.

*[GRANDMA enters stage right.]*

**GRANDMA:** Did I hear talk about being thankful?
**ANNIE:** *[smiles]* Grandma! Hi!
**CHUCK:** Hi Grandma. *[rubs hands together]* Did you bring the pies?
**GRANDMA:** *[laughs]* I sure did, one apple and one cherry.

ANNIE: No pumpkin?
GRANDMA: No, Annie. Your grandpa can't stand the smell of pumpkin pies baking.
ANNIE: That's OK. I love your cherry pie. And Dad loves apple!
CHUCK: *[looks a little sad and acts selfish]* Well, I'll miss the pumpkin.
GRANDMA: You can have a double slab of apple, Chuck! So what are you two thankful for this year?
ANNIE: Well, I passed my big math test yesterday. I'm *really* thankful for that.
CHUCK: Hmmm . . . I was planning on being thankful for pumpkin pie.
GRANDMA: I'll be very thankful when your grandfather finally gets here.
ANNIE: Why didn't he come with you?
GRANDMA: Oh, he had a few extra stops to make.
MOM: *[enters stage right]* I hope you're all hungry.
CHUCK: The turkey smells great, Mom.
ANNIE: Any cold pizza in the fridge?
MOM: *[laughs]* No, but I made your favorite corn casserole.
GRANDMA: There's sure no shortage of food to be thankful for around here.
MOM: *[lifts her head and looks offstage]* Uh oh, I think I hear the phone. Be right back.

*[MOM exits stage right]*

GRANDMA: Now Chuck, there must be something besides pumpkin pie to be thankful for, right?
CHUCK: Sure, Grandma, there's lots of things . . .
MOM: *[rushes back onstage and puts her hand on GRANDMA's arm]* Mom, we have to go. *[turns to ANNIE and CHUCK]* Your grandpa's in a little trouble, we won't be long.
GRANDMA: *[looks alarmed]* What's that man up to now?
MOM: He's not far away, let's go

*[MOM exits with GRANDMA stage right.]*

ANNIE: *[looks concerned]* I wonder if this is like last spring when Grandpa accidentally kicked the ladder over when he was on the roof?
CHUCK: Yeah, he yelled for an hour before somebody came.
ANNIE: Poor Grandpa!
CHUCK: I guess we're pretty lucky that Grandma and Grandpa can come over for Thanksgiving dinner.
ANNIE: Yeah, some of my friends don't have grandparents around at all.

Thankful for Pie

CHUCK: I guess I shouldn't complain about not having pumpkin pie. Grandma's an awesome cook!
ANNIE: I shouldn't complain either. At least we have a turkey and I do kind of like the white meat.

*[Laughter is heard from offstage. MOM and GRANDPA enter stage right. GRANDPA limps a little and MOM helps him to the couch.]*

ANNIE: What happened?
CHUCK: What happened? Are you OK Grandpa?
GRANDPA: Oh sure, but that big dog next door, Buster—
MOM: Buster just loves your grandpa, but he got so excited—
GRANDPA: He knocked me right onto the sidewalk. Good thing I had my cell phone!
MOM: Grandpa's knees quit working on him. But the happy part is—
GRANDPA: *[enters laughing, stage right, carrying pizza box and pie plate]* I saved the pies!
ANNIE and CHUCK: *[excitedly]* Pies?
GRANDPA: Well, I know how you kids are, so I got a pizza pie for Annie.
GRANDMA: *[sets pie down and opens pizza box]* Look Annie.
ANNIE: *[takes box]* It's shaped like a turkey! Thank you Grandpa *[hugs GRANDPA]*.
GRANDPA: And I got a pumpkin pie for Chuck.
GRANDMA: *[picks up pie and lifts foil]* Just for you kiddo.
CHUCK: Wow, thank you! *[peeks under foil]* Whipped cream too; this is the best!
MOM: Do you have cool grandparents or what?
ANNIE: *[sniffs turkey pizza]* I'll never complain about turkey again.
CHUCK: *[takes pie from GRANDPA]* I've never been so thankful in my life.
MOM: OK, now that we're all here safe and sound, I'll go wake up Dad. It's time to eat!
CHUCK: I'll say grace.
ANNIE: No, I'll say grace. I'm more thankful than you . . .
CHUCK: I don't *think* so . . .

*[ANNIE and CHUCK each take an elbow and help GRANDPA as they all exit. Blackout.]*